Biographies for Young Children

HARRIET TUBMAN
They Called Me Moses

Written by Linda D. Meyer
Illustrated by J. Kerstetter

Tubman

*The publisher would like to thank
Ellen Peterson at the Historical
Society of Delaware, and the
Reverend G.H. Carter at the
Harriet Tubman Home in Auburn,
New York.*

PREFACE

One of the beauties and one of the strengths of America is the diversity of nationalities and races. I once read that one may go to France, but not become French; go to Italy, and not become Italian; go to Germany, and not become German. But anybody who comes to America becomes an American. That truism makes me proud.

These peoples bring to America's shores the wealth of their own cultures, beliefs, dance, song and language, leaving us richer than before. It is far better, we believe, to celebrate the rainbow of humanity than it is to white wash it.

In HARRIET TUBMAN, we have made every effort to capture the essence of the black dialect, its charm and its effectiveness to convey meaning. It is our hope that we can instill in the children who read it an appreciation for its unique and lasting beauty. We are richer because it is part of us.

Linda D. Meyer

My name is Harriet Tubman. Though Daddy Ben and Mama Rit, they called me Hat. Other folks, they called me Moses.

I was born in Bucktown, Maryland, in a little log cabin. It weren't much, but Mama made it a good home for me and my ten brothers and sisters.

There was only one bad thing. Me and my people, we were slaves, and our Massa, Edward Brodas, he owned us. Now, people shouldn't own other people, but that's how it was then.

Life was hard. Sometimes the Massa would rent us out to other men who thought nothin' of workin' us in the fields till we were so tired, we dropped. And the whip, it hurt. They'd beat us. Seems hard to believe now. But that's how it was then.

Some of us couldn't take bein' slaves. It wasn't meant for one man to own another. And so we ran away.

One time a big black man took to runnin' for his freedom and the overseer was so mad he threw a heavy iron weight after him. I stood in the way, and the iron hit me in the head. It plum knocked me out. Don't know how long I slept, but after I woke I was never quite the same.

Maybe the Lord, He planned it. All I know is after I woke up, from that time on, I would fall asleep at the drop of a hat, and voices would come talk to me and tell me what I should do.

In 1844 I jumped the broom and married myself a freeman. John Tubman was his name. For four years we lived together happy.

The time come, though, when I had to go. It was time for me to run North to freedom. John, he didn't want to go. So I left by myself, and John I left behind.

It was 1849, and I couldn't be another man's property anymore. I had to run. I had to own myself. I couldn't say goodbye to my mama and daddy else they get in trouble with the Massa, but I sang a song under my sister's window to tell her what I had to do. I sang:

When the old chariot comes,
I'm going to leave you;
I'm bound for the promised land,
Friends, I'm going to leave you.

You see, the white people didn't know it, but when we black folk wanted to say something to each other, we sang it. And that was how we talked in the cotton fields.

So I ran North and when I ran, I hid in houses called "stations." These stations were run by people, often of the Quaker faith, who were called "station masters." I used the "Underground Railroad."

The Underground Railroad was a path black people took to go North to freedom and away from slavery.

I knew this work was for me: I would be a "conductor" on the Railroad. So I saved my money earned by cleanin' houses and doin' other folk's laundry, and when I had enough, I went back South. I found some other black people who wanted to be free, and I brought them North with me.

I'd sing a song like this under their windows:

When that there old chariot comes,
I'm going to leave you;
I'm bound for the promised land,
I'm going to leave you.

And they'd come out of their cabins and meet me, and I'd take them North with me so they could be free too.

All in all, they say I took over 300 slaves with me. I'd take anyone — women, children, old folks. Babies we'd give medicine to make them sleep.

They called me Moses, and they called me "Old Chariot." I don't care what they called me, as long as they didn't call me slave. Because I made myself a free woman.

My raids took to botherin' the white men so bad, they put dogs on my trail and money on my head. $40,000 it was. But no matter what they did, they never caught Harriet Tubman!

June 2, 1863, was a big day. I helped Colonel Montgomery, a Yankee soldier, save 750 slaves along the banks of the Combahee River. We rode a big boat by the shores, and my people, they came out and jumped on. Lordy, was that a sight!

Later on there came another way to free my people. The Civil War came, and I stopped my eight years of runnin' on the Railroad. During the war I cooked food and washed clothes and nursed hurtin' men. And when the Union Army asked me, I spied. Working together, we freed my people.

And there came a time I took myself another husband. March 18, 1869, it was, and Nelson Davis was his name.

After the war the blacks were free, but they didn't know how to be. So I worked with the Freedmen's Aid Society and we helped my people learn how to live again, this time in freedom.

Still later, poor people of all colors found their way to my door. I couldn't turn anyone away. I grew food and I begged clothes, and that way I took care of them. Later there were two homes: The Harriet Tubman Home and the Home for the Aged and Indigent.

It was a good life. I did what the Lord told me to
do. I never had no children of my own, though I did
take a niece to live with me. But it's no never mind. I
did what I had to do. And it was good.

INTRODUCING THE DECISION IS YOURS SERIES

These are fun books that help children age 7-11 think about social problems. Written in the "choose your own ending" format, the reader gets to decide what action the character will take and then gets to see the consequences of that decision.

These books:

- Address social issues, like stealing, jealousy, and lying, that affect 7-11 year olds.
- Encourage children to think about consequences.
- Help children develop and practice problem solving skills.
- Offer children a chance to see why some things work and some things don't.

FINDERS KEEPERS
by Elizabeth Crary

You and your friend Jerry are walking home from the pool on a hot summer day. You find a wallet lying under a tree — it belongs to your neighbor, Mr. French. Jerry wants to take a little money and buy ice cream. You're not sure what to do. Will you keep it? Will you turn it in? Will you go with Jerry to buy ice cream?

$3.95 paper,   64 pages, illustrated
ISBN 0-943990-38-6

BULLY ON THE BUS
by Carl W. Bosch

You had an argument with a big kid named Nick on the bus. Now Nick wants to beat you up. You don't want to fight, but you are tired of being hassled all the time. Your mom thinks you should ignore him and your best friend thinks you should move to Texas. You're not so sure either will work. What *will* you do?

$3.95 paper,   64 pages, illustrated
ISBN 0-943990-42-4

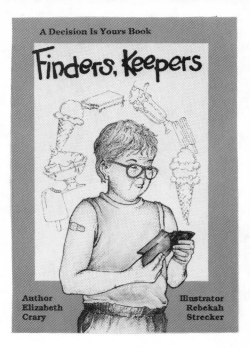

A Decision Is Yours Book

Finders, Keepers

Author Elizabeth Crary

Illustrator Rebekah Strecker

A DECISION IS YOURS BOOK

BULLY
on the bus

Written by Carl W. Bo
Illustrated by Rebekah J. S

6

You ask Jerry to give you the wallet so you ca take it to the pool. He says, "No!" You grab for th wallet and knock it from his hand.

Before you can pick up the wallet, Jerry standing with one foot on it. He flaps his arms li a bird and chants, "Chicken, chicken! You are chicken! You are a chicken!"

You are not sure what to do. Jerry says, "Cor on, it won't hurt you to look. I'm not going to ta anything."

If you decide to give it to the Lost and Found, tu to page

If you are curious to see if there is any money, tu to page

THE BIOGRAPHIES FOR YOUNG CHILDREN SERIES

Children make their decisions about male/female roles between the ages of 3-6. Because these ideas are formed so early, it is important for children to have examples of strong people who chose non-traditional roles and changed society. These picture-story books are fun and riveting for preschoolers and are simple enough for an eight year old to read alone.

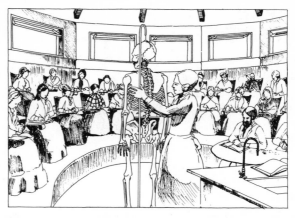

HARRIET TUBMAN: They Called Me Moses
by Linda Meyer
illustrated by J. Kerstetter

Harriet Tubman is probably the best remembered "conductor" on the Underground Railroad during the Civil War. The drama and adventure in her story will fascinate young children. Narrated by Harriet herself as a child.

$5.95 paper   32 pages, illustrated
ISBN 0-943990-32-7

COMING SOON:
JULIETTE GORDON LOW: Founder of the Girl Scouts
KATHARINE LEE BATES: Author of ''America the Beautiful''

ELIZABETH BLACKWELL: The Story of the First Woman Doctor
by Shari Steelsmith
illustrated by J. Kerstetter

Children will be interested to read about Elizabeth Blackwell's unusual childhood, fierce determination to become a doctor, hard work, various setbcks, and eventual success. Told from Elizabeth's viewpoint as a child.

$5.95, paper   32 pages, illustrated
ISBN 0-943990-30-0

Order Form

Bully on the Bus	$3.95	_____
Finders, Keepers	$3.95	_____
Elizabeth Blackwell	$5.95	_____
Harriet Tubman	$5.95	_____

Shipping

Order Subtotal	Shipping		
$ 0-$10	add $1.25	Subtotal	_____
$10-$25	add $2.25	Shipping	_____
$25-$50	add $3.25	*Sales Tax	_____
		Total	_____

* Washington state residents add 8.1%
Prices subject to change

Name _____

Address _____

City _____

State _____ Zip _____

Send check or money order to:
Parenting Press, Inc.
7744 31st Ave. NE
Suite 815
Seattle, WA 98115
or phone: **1-800-992-6657**

Volume Discounts Available